Skin, Bones, and
Too Much Love

Skin, Bones, and Too Much Love

-S.L. GRAY

ISBN-13: 978-1544652160

ISBN-10: 154465216X

For all the ones that 'You'
has belonged to.

I always thought
I was writing these words for me,
but within my soul I know
they were always meant for you to see.

I.

S.L. Gray

This was not searched for.

This was head down,
hands in pockets,
hurried steps,
and stumbling into something
I thought had indefinitely
left me behind.

This was the sweetest
sought after feeling
inside of an even sweeter soul
and I somehow
happening upon you.

There is nothing
about you that
I have once known.

But I was once told
what love was going
to feel like when
it finally came around
and in this way,

you are so familiar.

S.L. Gray

If I fall for you,
I pray for a long slow drop
without an ending.

Skin, Bones, and Too Much Love

I imagine you out there,
and it is like
lightning and thunder
in the distance.

I am mixed with
the excitement
for what is to come
and the want for you
to be so much closer.

S.L. Gray

I can promise you
there is no place waiting for you
more than my own arms.

There is so much
life to live still.

I cannot control
the pace in which
the moments will arrive.

I want to take on most things
that arrive carried in
by floods of light
at the slowest rate
that I can manage.

But you,
I think of living
these days with you
and I want in the same breath
to know every single one of them.

You have gone
into my head
hand in hand
with love.

I have never
known dreaming
like this.

Skin, Bones, and Too Much Love

Any walls
that I have created
to keep love out
have been destroyed
by my own desire
to get close to you.

S.L. Gray

I can be the silence
when the world around you
gets to be too loud.

I can be the rain
pattering on your rooftop
when you need that lullaby sound.

I can be anything
you want and need
to make this life settle in
and be at ease.

Before you touch me,
know that you
overwhelm me
and that I have
already crumbled.

When I saw you there,
in the depths of all you are
my heart found a home.

Skin, Bones, and Too Much Love

I am letting
my heart go to you.

It feels like
I set it off
running through
the dark.

I am unaware
of where
it is being lead to
or what will become of it.

But I know
with certainty
that I cannot possibly
call it back now.

S.L. Gray

My heart's so simple
it only wants just one thing:
to beat close to yours.

If there is any way
to describe the way
that I feel for you
it is that you are a book
filled with endless pages
of everything that
I have ever wished to know
and how I so desperately
wish to find a quiet place
and never put you down.

Anyone can give me love,
but it is only with you
in which I can return it.

I am here with you now.
Our cheeks are red and
our eyes are glowing.
I think it is you and
you believe it is me
that this light comes from,
for there was no light such as this
before this moment.
Lights were present, yes,
but this light is different,
(this life is different),
undeniably so.

S.L. Gray

It's always been yours,
I cannot find another
this heart will beat for.

You will always
be enough for me,
not even the greatest
dreamer could convince me
that there is more to life
than loving you.

S.L. Gray

Know that you
are enough for me,
but I will always
want more of you.

I realized
that I loved you
when I couldn't
be alone
in my thoughts
anymore.

The space
was no longer
my own, but ours.

S.L. Gray

You lean your head
into my shoulder
and I fall entirely into you.

Skin, Bones, and Too Much Love

My heart loves
that I am yours so much
that it has somehow
convinced my mind
to erase any memories
that I was ever anything else.

S.L. Gray

You have a soul
brighter than
anything in the sky.

To know you
is to gaze up
at the stars and
feel like they
couldn't possibly
give me a thing.

I like the
thought of you;
you make
my mind feel
beautiful.

S.L. Gray

You came into my life
unexpectedly,
but I hope you
never leave that way.

I will never be
somebody else's.
I will always be
either entirely yours
or completely my own.
There is nothing else
that I will ever find,
beyond you and I.

I have found nothing
more in this world that I want
since I have found you.

You've got it
right in the palm
of your hand
and it's beating
better than it ever
did in my chest.

S.L. Gray

You dove
into this ocean.
Still waters
are a faint
and ever fleeting
memory.

A world without you
is a slumber
without dreams.

S.L. Gray

I love you in ways
hopeless romantics
want to be loved
and I hold you in ways
the moon wishes
it could with the sun.

Skin, Bones, and Too Much Love

I have heard stories
of hearts half-full.

Stories of hearts
too unfortunate to have
ever been touched
by a heart like yours.

My heart sits satisfied
in my chest
filled with love
for you and from you.

I have no empty space
that aches for anything more.

S.L. Gray

Your eyes light up
and that is my way home.

My feelings are sewn into
the seams of yours.

The sun is shining on you
at this very moment,
and I can feel its warmth
on my own skin.

Should your world
ever crumble,
we will both feel the shake.

S.L. Gray

There are many ways
to love and be loved and
with you, I have found it all.

There isn't any type of love
that I cannot find in you.

And when I love you
so much of it pours out of me
that it feels like
in all the ways to love someone,
I have given them all to you.

I was never lonely
until I stumbled
into your company
and now all I want
is for my silence
to be filled with you.

S.L. Gray

I would fight against
the hands of time to have more
than forever with you.

I have never been able
to shut you out;
you come and go
from a place inside
of my heart that is
only known to you.

S.L. Gray

We share the same darkness.

I hope that can only mean
that we will find the same light.

Skin, Bones, and Too Much Love

Time speaks in my ear
that you are taking too long.

Tries to put the fear in me
that I am going to grow old
and still be waiting for you.

But time does not know
that I will wait for you
no matter how much
it etches itself into my skin,
for time spent with anyone else
would be the waste of it.

Whenever you are ready
I will still be ready too.

S.L. Gray

Time can change a lot of things
but never my mind about you.

Before you,
love could have
been anything
but now love is
defined by all
the ways that
I have been
loved by you.

S.L. Gray

I will always
be here for you,
even when it feels
like you only want me
when you need me.
Even when it feels
wrong of me to allow
you to take from me
without a thought
to give me any parts
of yourself to replace
all that you have taken.
I will always
be here for you;
until you have
all that you want from me.

If you stay
here with me
or I with you

I don't see
those dark clouds
dissipating

I see them
building and
rushing towards us

but you know
I have always had
a thing for that
kind of weather.

S.L. Gray

My greatest fear
is within losing you
and having to settle
my heart is a place
where I will feel like
I do not belong.

Skin, Bones, and Too Much Love

I cannot walk
away from you;

I am still falling into
everything that you are.

I cannot take one step
in a new direction
until you have given me
solid ground to plant my feet upon
and even then, I am certain

I would climb back up
everything that you are
and fall again.

S.L. Gray

I may not always
be in love with you,
but I will always
know love
when I think of you.

Should this rose
ever wilt
please remember
how I cut off
its thorns.

My only intention
was to love you
and nothing more.

II.

I think of your hands
and how they must
constantly ache terribly
to reach out and touch
the one you have
fallen deeply in love with
and cannot have.

In this silence,
I cannot figure out
whether you have given up
or have found all
that you've been
searching for.

S.L. Gray

We couldn't
have always stayed
in the same place.

We were always
going to move
in some direction.

It was at first
quickly towards
each other
and then slowly
slowly away.

Maybe the world
couldn't handle a love
as deep as ours,
so fate tore us apart
to save humanity.

Maybe this is for the best.

S.L. Gray

I won't ever forget you,
and maybe that is
the only forever
the two of us together
were ever meant to have.

For you and I,
time had never been
more selfish.

S.L. Gray

We started falling apart
and I could not
show my strength.

Because I told you
I would never
hold you back

and even though
it feels like
the only thing my arms
were ever meant to do
is hold you,

I had to put them
to my sides
and let you go.

You are gone,
and I will miss you
for as long
as I told you
I would love you.

S.L. Gray

It is impossible
for someone like you
to go away and not
have someone waiting
around for your return.

Time will be measured.

There will always be
fresh steps in all
the places that
you were last seen.

If all I become to you
is nothing but a memory,
I hope you'll let me breathe
by thinking of me.

S.L. Gray

Neither one of us changed
but you and I as one did.

You were everything
I ever wanted
and everything I knew
I could not have.

You are often smiling
inside of my head
but never in my direction.

I can see light
shining everywhere,
but I am never
blinded by it.

S.L. Gray

My mind knows
I cannot have you,
but that doesn't
stop it from dreaming
of all the ways
that I could.

I am still
silently hoping
that time has
made a mistake
and has already
reserved a moment
for us to find
each other again.

S.L. Gray

There are things
you have never touched
and places you
have never been
and still, somehow
I find you in them all.

I'll spend the forever
you promised me
trying to forget
what will never be.

S.L. Gray

I need to think
of you
and the beginning;

otherwise,

I will forget why
it was worth it
to have let what was
once whole become
so torn apart.

I still think
love wanted you
to be with me.

S.L. Gray

Love comes around
carried in the arms
of others that cannot
hold me the way you did.

I dream of
seeing you again,
and it is just
you and me
everything that
stood in our way
cannot find us there.

S.L. Gray

I wish I saw you
more than just
in my dreams,
I don't want to
believe that is the
only world where
you can exist with me.

Missing you
is something that
I will never get over
I cannot walk this earth
and not notice that
it is entirely empty.

S.L. Gray

I have late night conversations
with the moon,
he tells me about the sun
and I tell him about you.

What would you
say or think
if you knew
how stuck
I am in the past?

In my mind
you tell me that time
cannot move you
forward either.

You tell me
that we carry
the weight of
the same years
on our shoulders.

(I know I am
wasting daydreams.
I know I am
coming across as selfish)

S.L. Gray

I know that people change.
Nothing ever stays the same.
Every day our bodies age older
and something will be done to us
to cause a change on the inside.

But you are so different that
I almost didn't recognize you,
and when we spoke
I wasn't surprised
to find a change in your thoughts,
but at myself
for feeling a hope
I didn't know I carried
die within me.

A hope that everything
inside of you
had frozen in place for me.

There is a hollow space
very stubborn within me
wanting only you.

S.L. Gray

I will always wonder
what life would have been
if I lived it with you.

I imagine there would
have been light.

I imagine that all
the love in the world
would have come
rushing to our door
to be used by us.

Skin, Bones, and Too Much Love

My bedroom window faces the sun,
which is much too bright
for just waking out of sleep.
So I replaced my white curtains
with blackout ones.
The sun still shines through
around the edges of the curtains
as if to say, *"I'm still here"*,
and I thought about my own heart
and how I haven't told you
that my love for you is the sun
and that it is much too bright
inside of someone who can't have you.
How I have tried to cover it up
with just about everything
and that no matter what
you are still here.

S.L. Gray

I am still picking
pieces of you
out of my memory.

Just when I thought
I had finally forgotten you,
sleep took over,
and we were dancing again.

S.L. Gray

You are not someone
that gets forgotten
and neither someone
that needs a reminder
to be remembered.

I care about you
a lot more
than our circumstances
allow me to.

S.L. Gray

In the blink of an eye
I loved you.

I lost you seemingly
just as fast.

I opened my eyes
to find hurt
and I have been
blinking ever since,

but it never goes.

It is always the first
thing I find.

Skin, Bones, and Too Much Love

This isn't the first time
the overwhelming urge
to seek you out
has woken me up at 3 a.m.

I am fighting to keep still;
to keep from running to a place
where the open sign
is merely a flickering light,
and the exit sign is blinding.

You have the
warmest embrace
that I, a guest, tried
to make a home out of
only to break apart
my own structure

Tonight I will save
all that has been rebuilt
and keep myself from
feeling the grip of regret
that always pulled me away.

S.L. Gray

Some nights
it is all too much,
and I start to seriously
become sorry
that I ever discovered
any part of you.

No one should be able
to make missing someone
feel like actual hunger.

I've no appetite
to be whole on my own
and for that, I must be sorry.

I am becoming tired.
So tired of you
coming back
in the wrong way.

I want you physically
right next to me,
dreams come easier.
These old memories
lay next to me
and keep me up all night.

This has been going on
for too long.

The clock just changed
to the first hour of morning.
You come back again
in the way I cannot hold you.

It's too late in the night for this.
It's too late in my life for this.

How very selfish of me
to wish to forget you,
but for you to remember me
no matter how hard
you wish to forget me.

Skin, Bones, and Too Much Love

They said you're happy again.

They didn't say what it was
that found its way into your world
and warmed that spot next to you
that had always been mine.

They didn't have to tell me
that you aren't alone
and that your hands
are being gentle again.

But you aren't,
and they are, aren't they?

I am trying my best
to settle that thought
in nicely here,
but it is an animal,
and it is wild and biting.

S.L. Gray

You should be happy.

Right now there is so much
bitterness and hurt
piled upon my good nature.

Underneath of it all,
I really do
wish you the best.

I won't dwell too long here.

Just give me enough time
to take one last good look
at all that we were
until the damage set itself in
and became unmovable.

The moments of us
that will always be gentle with me
are certainly salvageable,
and I will let them continue
to live in me.

I'll gather together the rest,
make peace with it all,
and bury it.

I'll move on.
Just give me enough time.

S.L. Gray

One day
I'll have enough gut
to get you off my chest.

I regret the end.

The way we couldn't
leave one another
without wounds.

The way we made
it seem as if
all the love we shared
was wasted time.

S.L. Gray

You go.

You have gone so many times
that I am becoming
more familiar with that action
and what is left after
than I am with your presence.

So, keep going.

Soon enough
it will lose its strength
to cause me any harm,
and there will be nothing
here for you to come back to,

nothing you can leave again.

I cannot pinpoint
how far you have gone.

But my dreams
of you have been few,

and they are like
messages that have been
written in the sand
too close to the shoreline.

*I think you have gone
quite far.*

S.L. Gray

You are no longer
home to me.

You are still
a home to me.

Just an old one
that no longer holds
anything for me
to return to.

There was a moment,
(more than enough time),
when you could have
come back, and everything
would still have been yours
for the taking.

But every feeling
left alone long enough will fade.

You reappear
and are recognized still
but everything here,
every single thing,
belongs to me again.

S.L. Gray

I have nothing to say
about you anymore
it has been so long
since I have seen you
I am not so sure
the person I'd speak of
is you any longer.

I can still feel everything
that I have ever felt for you,
but it breathes easier in me
as if it has all gone into
a quiet slumber to rest
until you return and wake them.

S.L. Gray

Just promise
to remember me
when you find
yourself in all
the places that
I will never be.

I remember you,
and it doesn't hurt
to do that anymore.

S.L. Gray

Don't give up on love;
one day you will find all the right ways
to hold the stem of a rose.

We don't get to choose
what is done to us.
We do, however, get to choose
how long it is done to us.

You can choose
to wither
or you can choose
to grow.

S.L. Gray

Treat love like a plant;
you cannot rush its growth.

and I hope the right
kind of love gets to you
before the wrong ones
leave you in pieces
and keep you from
accepting what is real.

The day you decide
to be yourself
is the day a path
will be cleared
and everything
that is truly meant for you
will finally start
their journey to find you.

I hope you never
waste a moment of your life
afraid to change it.

S.L. Gray

Be broken
but still love easy
like you are
breathing in air.

And though your heart
may feel like it is
black and blue
still love like it is
beating vibrantly red.

There are people
who are going to be
everything you want
and they will not
be bad for you.

You will find them.

S.L. Gray

And there is that light
you never saw arising.

How it crashes into you
and makes you feel alive,
makes you want to live.

It happens suddenly.
I hope it happens to you.

Skin, Bones, and Too Much Love

The wrong ones
will tell you
you are too much.

The right ones
will tell you
you are an adventure.

S.L. Gray

Tomorrow will come.

To travel lighter,

you should leave
the hurt behind.

It is unavoidable
when you know
that your happiness
is waiting
in some other place.

Somewhere far off
that makes where
you are lose all its color.

It is okay to leave
everything behind
and go there.

S.L. Gray

You give all
your pieces away
and wonder why
you fall apart.

Sometimes
you are unaware
that you are
the one doing
the ruining.

S.L. Gray

Hurt is so small
compared to love
when they sit
in the same hand.

We often
(if not always)
miss it.

Let go.

It is impossible
for a heart
to breathe in
an atmosphere
where the air
is no longer
being provided.

S.L. Gray

Fall apart
to separate yourself
from the pain.

All we want
is for a single soul
to see who we are
in the darkness
and not reach
for a light.

S.L. Gray

To let another life tell you
how your own should be lived
is like choosing to live beneath
artificial light instead of the sun.

You were a light
before you ever
lit up their darkness.

S.L. Gray

Hold onto the parts
of yourself
that you love the most.

They are too good
for everyone.

Please do not
plant your love
in a heart
that has no sun.

S.L. Gray

Do not let anyone
make you believe
that their heart
is the only heart
that will love yours.

Where their
love ends
is not the ending
to all love.

One heart
does not speak
for the rest of us.

There is nothing wrong
with the way you love.
We have all had moments
of picking the wrong flowers
to rain our love upon.

They hold you simply
because you are already
in their reach.

They cling to your soul
only in fear that they
will not get their hands
on another.

They do not get to keep you.

You deserve to be held
with love.

If anyone is going
to get their hands
on your soul,
they need to belong
to someone who wants
to know every single thing
that it is made of.

She would always throw
her heart into war
even if she didn't know
what it was fighting for.

S.L. Gray

If she does not send
a tidal wave of shivers
down your spine,
then please do not
stand in her ocean
and waste her time.

Even with half a heart,
she would still love so deeply
the world thought
she was perfectly whole.

S.L. Gray

You have always been lovely,
even when the wrong ones
got to have you in their lives
and made you feel like you were not.

My mother told me
when I was born
she was repaid
all the love
she was never given.

I will always love
I was made for it.

S.L. Gray

There is nothing
that can stop me
from living this life.

I have looked up
to a woman constantly
showing me
how it is done.

The sweet days will come
once you let go of all the things
that will keep going.

S.L. Gray

I have become someone
who enjoys letting things go.

There is this peace
after forgiveness
that I have discovered.

It is lovely and sweet,
and no amount
of pain will ever stop me
from returning to it

Sometimes I don't want
to come home to myself.
Sometimes it is hard
to love being there.

But I always return,
always,
to let myself be aware
of the lovely things
that have grown here
and the lovely things
that have yet to arrive.

To make a promise
that if ever given the chance
I will not abandon this body
for any other.

I will take care of myself.

I will not always be troubled
with what I find here.

I dream and they tell me
I am out of my mind.

As if there is a better way.

S.L. Gray

I used to fall for skin
now I am falling for souls.

I admit that
certain souls
make me weak.

I am always
willing to make
a terrible mess
of myself with them.

S.L. Gray

I am made up of nothing
but skin, bones, and
too much love.

I am cleaning
this heart up.

Not so someone else
will come across it
and find that they
can love it,

but because it is time
that I start to.

S.L. Gray

I am more of a threat
to my own heart
than anyone else could be.

I owe most
of my ability
to hope to the ones
I cannot turn away
who only bring rain
for regrowth.

S.L. Gray

If you're going to call me beautiful,
I hope I do not find that your eyes
are crafting a memory of my body,
for the beauty of what I am on the outside
will someday fade away.
I am not the skin that I have been sewn into
if you are going to say those words to me
I want them to mean
that you have taken the time
to dig deeply into who I am on the inside
and have seen every part of me
that the sun cannot breathe light upon,
what may be broken and what may be whole
and "You're beautiful," are the words
you could not help but let escape you
and let do what the sun cannot.

I want something
to be found within me
when I have nothing at all.

To know that
I alone am enough
even on the days
when I feel as empty
as a tree whose leaves
have gone in the fall.

S.L. Gray

I am full of want.

I am often finding myself aware
that it is hard to be of this kind.

I want
and want and want
until it leaves me breathless
and aching from running
after it all.

But I dream in color
awake and asleep.

And sometimes I am met
halfway through running,
and I hold and am held
by the most beautiful things.

It is hard to be of this kind
but so very worth it.

My heart does not know
the method in which to turn
its love into hate.

S.L. Gray

There is this strength
that hides within me.

I have lost the things
I said that I lived for
and have continued to live.

My heart is
forever heavy.

I let everything in
with no intention
to let anything out.

S.L. Gray

Here's to us.

The ones caught
too easily,

the ones with
no defense,

the ones
much too vulnerable
when love
presents itself.

Acknowledgments

Thank you to my incredible mother for giving me too much love.

Thank you to all my readers for the never ending kind words and support I needed to write this.

Thank you. Thank you. Thank you.

Other places to find S.L. Gray:

Instagram: @s.l._gray
Tumblr: slgraywords

Made in the USA
Columbia, SC
16 October 2018